CITIZENSHIP

WITHDRAWN

by Lucia Raatma

CHERRY LAKE PUBLISHING * ANN ARBOR, MICHIGAN

Published in the United States of America by Cherry Lake Publishing
Ann Arbor, Michigan
www.cherrylakepublishing.com

Reading Consultant: Cecilia Minden-Cupp, PhD, Literacy Consultant

Photo Credits: Cover and page 4, © iStockphoto.com/Lisay; page 6, © Jim West/Alamy; cover
and page 8, © iStockphoto.com/robcruse; cover and page 10, © Richard A. McGuirk, used under
license from Shutterstock, Inc.; page 12, © David R. Frazier Photolibrary, Inc.; page 14, © MaxFX,
used under license from Shutterstock, Inc.; cover and page 16, © Frontpage, used under license from
Shutterstock, Inc.; page 18, © Rob Byron, used under license from Shutterstock, Inc.; page 20,
© Marmaduke St. John/Alamy

LIBRARY OF CONGRESS CATALOGING-IN-PUBLICATION DATA
Raatma, Lucia.
 Citizenship / by Lucia Raatma.
    p. cm.—(Character education)
 Includes bibliographical references and index.
 ISBN-13: 978-1-60279-324-8
 ISBN-10: 1-60279-324-7
 1. Citizenship—Juvenile literature. I. Title. II. Series.
 JF801.R32 2009
 323'.6—dc22   2008031262

Cherry Lake Publishing would like to acknowledge the work of
The Partnership for 21st Century Skills.
Please visit www.21stcenturyskills.org for more information.

CONTENTS

Do you have any neighbors you can help?

What Is Citizenship?

"Can you help my mom and me raise money for the hospital?" Liza asked when her neighbor opened the door.

"Of course!" said Mrs. Black. She handed Liza's mom some money.

"Thanks," Liza said. "I'd be happy to help you rake leaves later."

"You're a good **citizen**, Liza. I'm glad we're neighbors," Mrs. Black said with a smile.

Cleaning up around your school is one way to help your community.

A good citizen helps make the world a better place. This means helping your family, **community**, and planet.

Good citizens know their actions affect others. They try to make good choices in everything they do.

Recycling is easy after you learn how to do it.

Being a Good Citizen

There are many ways to be a good citizen. You can do your chores at home. You can **recycle** bottles, cans, and paper. You can pick up trash on your street. These actions show that you care about your home and your community.

Create!

Sit down with your family. Make a list of the ways you can help your community. Think of materials you can recycle. Include ways to save water, gas, and electricity. Put the list in a spot where you will see it often.

Raking leaves is just one chore you can do to help a neighbor. Your neighhbor will be happy you helped!

You can be a good citizen by helping people in your neighborhood. Maybe an older neighbor needs help with yard work or walking a pet. Maybe you can water plants for a neighbor who is on vacation.

You can also help clean up a local park. This won't just help one person. It will make your community better for everyone.

Be a good school citizen at lunchtime. Invite new kids to eat with you. Clean up when you are done eating.

You can show good citizenship at school by trying to make it better. Do you see things that need fixing? Report them to the office.

Is there a new student in your class? You can help him feel welcome. Invite him to eat lunch with you and your friends. Include him in a game at recess.

Do you stop at stop signs when you ride your bike? Good citizens follow laws to help keep everyone safe.

You can be a good citizen in your community. One way is to obey the laws. Don't litter. Never hurt or take someone else's property.

Tell an adult if you see other people breaking the law. Our communities are safer when everyone follows the laws.

Ask Questions!

Write down two rules that you must follow at home. Then ask two friends to name two rules that they must follow at home. Were any of the rules your friends named the same as your family's rules?

Good citizens learn about candidates and vote in elections. You can't vote yet, but you can start learning about how elections work.

Spreading Citizenship

Being a good citizen means keeping up with what is happening in your community. Ask your parents or teachers about **candidates** who are running for office. You aren't old enough to vote yet. But you can start learning about how leaders are elected.

People who like animals often volunteer their time at animal shelters.

Many people show their good citizenship by getting involved with local **charities**. Some people **volunteer** their time at an animal shelter. Others take part in a run or walk to raise money. Find out what you can do to help. Then do your part to pitch in.

Crossing guards help kids follow safety rules. How can you help someone be a good citizen today?

Think about where you live. Show good citizenship. Do your part to make your world better. Other people **appreciate** it when you are a good citizen. Your actions may help them be good citizens, too!

Think!

Imagine that no one in your town was a good citizen. No one obeyed the laws. No one worked together or helped one another. What would it be like to live in that town?

GLOSSARY

appreciate (uh-PREE-shee-ate) to value or enjoy someone or something

candidates (KAN-duh-dates) people who are applying for a job or running in an election

charities (CHAYR-uh-teez) groups that raise money and help people in need

citizen (SIH-tuh-zun) someone who lives in a certain town or country

community (kuh-MYOO-nuh-tee) a group of people who live in the same area or who have something in common with one another

recycle (ree-SYE-kuhl) to process old items so they can be used to make new products

volunteer (vol-uhn-TIHR) to offer to do a job for no pay

FIND OUT MORE

BOOKS

Small, Mary. *Being a Good Citizen.* Mankato, MN: Picture Window Books, 2006.

Suen, Anastasia. *Vote for Isaiah! A Citizenship Story.* Edina, MN: Looking Glass Library, 2008.

WEB SITES

Be a Volunteer
kidshealth.org/kid/feeling/thought/volunteering.html
Learn more about volunteering

The Democracy Project— Inside the Voting Booth
pbskids.org/democracy/vote/index.html
Learn more about voting and how one person's vote can make a difference

INDEX

ABOUT THE AUTHOR

Lucia Raatma has written dozens of books for young readers. They are about famous people, historical events, ways to stay safe, and other topics. She lives in Florida's Tampa Bay area with her husband and their two children.